MIND
MAN
AND
MACHINE

A DIALOGUE

Second Edition

Paul T. Sagal

Hackett Publishing Company, Inc.

Indianapolis/Cambridge

First edition copyright © 1982 by Paul T. Sagal
Second edition copyright © 1994 by Paul T. Sagal

00 99 98 97 96 95 94   1 2 3 4 5 6 7

For further information, please address
  Hackett Publishing Company, Inc.
  P.O. Box 44937
  Indianapolis, Indiana 46244-0937

Design by Dan Kirklin

Library of Congress Cataloging-in-Publication Data
Sagal, Paul T.
   Mind, man, and machine: a dialgoue/Paul T. Sagal.—2nd ed.
        p.   cm.
Includes bibliographical references.
ISBN 0-87220-264-X (alk. paper). ISBN 0-87220-263-1 (paper: alk. paper)
1. Philosophy—Introductions. I. Title.
BD21.S24   1994
128' .2—dc20   94-21166
                                                                  CIP

The paper used in this publication meets the minimum requirements
of American National Standard for Information Sciences—Permanence
of Paper for Printed Library Materials, ANSI Z39.48-1984.

Mind
Man
and
Machine

Second Edition

Preface

It is a pleasure, both intellectual and otherwise, to have the opportunity to revise *Mind, Man, and Machine* after more than ten years. It gives me a chance to make some necessary corrections and clarifications, as well as improvements, to the dialogue—improvements based on developments from the rather vast philosophical literature on the topics covered in *Mind, Man, and Machine* since the time of its writing; on the comments of readers, teachers, and students who have read and studied the book; and on my own somewhat sporadic thinking and rethinking of the material during the past ten years, in which I have used the book regularly in my introductory philosophy classes. There seems to be a consensus that there are a number of good things about *Mind, Man, and Machine*: its being both accessible to relatively unsophisticated philosophy students and enjoyable, even at times humorous, reading; its focus on the Gödel-Church-Lucas argument—and its attempt to render this argument as simply as possible; and its rather wide range of

v

subject, from mind/body and other minds to free will, treated in a "little" book. In the second edition I try to preserve these putative good things. The chief modifications and additions are the following: 1) I have tried to make it clear that what I term the Gödel-Church argument against mechanism is really the well-known, controversial argument of British philosopher J. R. Lucas. Hence, I usually refer to it as the Gödel-Church-Lucas argument. 2) John Searle's influential _Chinese Room_ argument, a philosophically and pedagogically useful sequel to Turing's imitation game argument, is presented in a somewhat simplified version and is discussed so as to take into account some of the important criticisms of Searle's conclusion in the philosophical literature. This critical discussion, it turns out, was quite close to that followed in this dialogue. 3) A new argument based somewhat loosely on Tarski's work on truth and the liar paradox is offered by Phil to show that contra-Lucas man is actually _inferior_ to machines. The argument is offered not so much for its own sake as to give the reader additional practice in handling some of the basic concepts of the previous Gödel-Church discussion. 4) I have added a passage of dialogue dealing with the problem of _qualia_, qualitative features of experience like color properties, in an attempt to focus on what may be the crucial problem for mechanism. Frank Jackson's famous essay _What Mary Didn't Know_ is the focus of this discussion, but the approach taken is, I believe, somewhat original, or at least unusual. I also take into account D. C. Dennett's recent and influential response defending the mechanist line against Jackson's argument. There are many other changes, most of them small and most of them aimed at clarification or removal of infelicities. I am reasonably certain that the second edition is a genuine improvement—how much of an improvement must be left to the reader to judge. I would like to thank my colleagues Richard Ketchum and Timothy Cleveland for their participation in recent discussions of the topics covered in the dialogue. All blunders, obscurities, and embarrassments are, of course, my own. To the editorial staff of Hackett, I am especially grateful for constructive suggestions and criticisms and for other help.

My thanks to Tina Lujan for help with the typescript.

In memory of George Berry

To Karen

MIND
MAN
AND
MACHINE

Mind
Man
and
Machine

Participants:

STU
PHIL
MATT

The First Day

Stu has returned from a session of the U.S. Open chess tournament, where he has just lost his game to computer Fischkov III.

STU: I hate to lose—but especially to computers. How can they outthink me when they can't even think?

PHIL: What makes you so positive they can't think? Maybe more things can think than you think.

STU: You must be joking. Computers can no more think than parrots or phonograph records. Parrots and phonograph records just make sounds. There's no thought behind the sounds.

1

PHIL: But how do you know there's no thought behind the sounds? How can you tell when thinking is taking place?

STU: I'm sure I can tell when *I'm* thinking. It's as if I can hear the sounds of myself thinking. Maybe thinking is a kind of talking to oneself, a kind of self-talk.

PHIL: How do you know there is thought behind those "sounds" you hear? And how could you ever tell that I'm thinking? You can't *hear* my self-talk, can you? How do you even know it's going on?

STU: I can ask you.

PHIL: OK, but if you do ask, and I answer Yes, what can you do to check my answer? Perhaps if you asked Polly whether she was talking to herself, she'd also say *Yes*.

STU: Well, it's not merely the talk or even the self-talk that's thinking. It's the thought processes that accompany it, processes like conceptualization, reasoning, and things like that.

PHIL: First of all let me point out that even when I observe myself thinking, there is usually more than talking going on; there is picturing or imagining. I think about my last fishing trip. I "see" the cabin by the lake. At the same time, I'm talking to myself about the cabin. But you now say there is more to thinking than all this. There is what some people call "the higher mental processes." Let me ask you this. Do you ever observe yourself conceptualizing?

STU: Not really.

PHIL: So how do you know you conceptualize at all?

STU: How could I use concepts unless I somehow formed them?

PHIL: So you *infer* the existence of these mental acts. But explain to me what you mean by *using concepts*. How do you use concepts?

STU: When I make judgments about chairs or gila monsters, I use the concepts *chair* and *gila monster*.

PHIL: Why not just say that you know how to use the terms "chair" and "gila monster." Couldn't we really do without all this psychobabble about concepts and conceptualization and simply speak of learning and using a language? Then the interesting question would be whether machines can learn and use a language. If they can, your main objection to machine thinking would seem to evaporate.

STU: I can see what you're driving at. It does seem clearer when we talk about language use rather than concepts. If there's one thing a chess connoisseur like me appreciates, it's clarity. Still, I don't believe you've made clear to me what thinking is. Does every use of language involve thinking? Parrots seem to use language, but they don't think, do they? Not all use of language is thoughtful—or is it only the *thoughtful* use of language that really counts as *use of language*? We seem to be running around in circles—defining *thinking* in terms of the use of language and explaining the use of language in terms of the *thoughtful* use of language. I admit that I didn't begin where I should have begun, that is, with a definition of thought or thinking. But I don't see that you've supplied such a definition either.

PHIL: Yes, ideally speaking we should begin with a definition. But there are different kinds of definitions. Philosophers have been occupied with definitions since the time of Socrates. Socrates asked such ambitious questions as What is justice? What is virtue? What is knowledge? For our purposes, or to answer Socrates' questions, can we simply consult the dictionary? Dictionary or lexical definitions don't usually provide the clarification we're after. The dictionary is likely to give us something similar to the list of synonyms we began with. The defining terms would themselves be in equal need of definition. Of course we can't go on defining forever. But we do need to stop at a place more intelligible than where we began. What do we want from our definition of *thinking*? I think we would want a definition that would be useful in providing criteria, a combination of verifiably necessary and sufficient conditions, for identifying thinking. After all, we want to know whether *Fischkov III* or other such machines can think, so we need some kind of test procedure. If we're going to use such terms as *conceptualize* and *reason*, those terms must be tied to some observational or verifiable criteria. When possible it's best to speak in terms of the concrete—that is, talking, conducting a conversation, performing calculations.

STU: If what you're after is some kind of practical or practicable definition of thinking, I agree. I'm still quite sure, however, that machines do not think. *Fischkov III* beat me, but he—I mean *it,*—did no thinking. I didn't do *enough* thinking, but victor *Fischkov* didn't think at all.

PHIL: But you will admit that we need criteria to tell whether you are right. Your claim would have to be restated thus: According to acceptable criteria a, b, c of thinking, *Fischkov* did not think.

STU: OK, you give me the criteria.

PHIL: I can't give them to you. We must agree on them together. Then we can evaluate your claim about the chess-playing computer. You're sure that *Fischkov* doesn't think; apparently for you, then, *playing* good chess is not a sufficient criterion for the presence of thinking.

STU: I would no more say that *Fischkov* thinks than that a simple adding machine thinks. *Fischkov* simply calculates many moves ahead. I'd be a much better chess player if I could calculate as far ahead as *Fischkov* can.

PHIL: What exactly do you do in *your* chess playing that *Fischkov* doesn't do?

STU: I play with plans, with strategic goals, and with tactical devices to achieve them effectively.

PHIL: And how do you know you have these plans and goals and devices? Is it again a matter of your talking to yourself about these things?

STU: Pretty much.

PHIL: Then how do you know *Fischkov* isn't talking to himself about these things? Can't you infer his thinking from his playing?

STU: Here is where I have you. I've seen *Fischkov's* program, and all *Fischkov* does is calculate: If my opponent moves here and then I move here, if he moves here and then I move here, he captures my queen. So much for that option and others like it. It's all purely mechanical.

PHIL: At least, *Fischkov* has to know that losing the queen is bad. *Fischkov* has to do something more than calculate—he has to evaluate. So *Fischkov* attaches values to states of affairs.

STU: But *Fischkov* doesn't decide on minority attacks or king-side attacks or prophylaxis à la Nimzowitch.

PHIL: And if *Fischkov* could answer questions about strategic concepts such as those you just mentioned, would you admit that *Fischkov* thinks? At least you don't believe that thinking or successful thinking in chess involves some mysterious, miraculous inner process.

STU: I'm afraid I still can't shake my belief in those inner processes. You've been trying to take me further and further away from the value of introspection, but I'm not sure I should let you.

PHIL: OK, let's talk a bit more about this. Suppose there are some inner, introspectively available requirements of thinking. You have no access to these phenomena with respect to other thinking beings. You can't get inside my head, but I take it you believe that I think. And, on the basis of behavioral criteria, you surely deny that rosebushes think. So why do we need to get into this question of inner processes at all? Of course I admit there remains the hard question about the relation between the inner processes and the behavioral criteria.

STU: For the time being I will admit that if *Fischkov* could successfully manipulate strategic concepts . . .

PHIL: You mean if his program contained strategic terms, or if on the basis of his program and playing we could attribute certain strategic concepts to it.

STU: OK, have it your way. If what you say is true, I will admit that *in some sense* machines like *Fischkov* can think. But look, we are versatile thinkers, we are more than chess players. Our thinking in chess is related to our thinking in other areas. The special-purpose kind of thinking present in chess may be simulated by a machine, but it is just not enough to characterize thinking in general. Playing chess or the potential to play might be a necessary condition for thinking, but it is not enough. Human thinking must be versatile, it must be applicable to very different situations. Chess planning is one thing, but planning in general is another. Just because a machine can play chess, even if it can adequately answer questions about how it plays chess, it does not follow that it can think, or at least think like us. Thinking requires more complex behavior than does chess playing.

PHIL: Then if chess doesn't do the trick, we need some other way to establish criteria which optimally would provide necessary and sufficient conditions for thinking. We've admitted, I think, that if X plays chess (at a certain level) in a certain way, then X thinks to some extent. A mathematician named Turing suggested a more ambitious game which if played successfully by a machine would confirm that the machine thinks. It is, according to Turing, both necessary and sufficient for a machine's thinking that it compete successfully in his game. He calls this game the imitation game.[1] Let's see if you would be willing to play his game. The imitation game is a contest between a human being, A, and a computer, B. Questions are submitted to A and B, and it is A's task to convince some judge C that he or she, A, is the human being, and B's task to get C to make the wrong identification or to be unable to make any identification. It would be both unfair and unnecessary to allow C to view A and B. After all, what do looks have to do

1. A. N. Turing, "The Imitation Game," in A. R. Anderson, ed. *Minds and Machines* (Englewood Cliffs, N.J.: Prentice-Hall, 1964).

with the answers to our questions? We don't want to discriminate against B because it has an "ugly," machinelike appearance. So we place A and B behind a screen. We also let A and B type or print out the responses, so that the appearance of the response doesn't give away who's who. Note that this game requires much more of the machine than that it play chess; it will have to deal here with a wide range of questions. Don't you agree that if you could conduct an intelligent discussion with a machine, it would be foolish to deny that it could think?

STU: Are there really machines that can play the imitation game successfully?

PHIL: That's not quite the point. Even if there are no machines that can compete right at this moment, the likelihood or even the possibility of there being such in the future would force you to concede the possibility of a computer's thinking. It should no longer make you shudder at claims of such achievement.

STU: It looks as though I have to concede the possibility of a kind of crucial experiment to decide whether machines can think. But I still feel there's something fishy about the imitation game. I'm not sure that playing the game successfully is an acceptable criterion for thinking. Let me see if I can explain myself. What would computer success in the imitation game actually prove? It would only show that a computer can be programmed to accomplish the imitation. When we think, when real thinking takes place, nothing is rigged to imitate anything. It's like a point I raised in connection with *Fischkov*. There is something more involved here than outcomes. A tape recorder can successfully imitate a human voice; the outcome is the same, but it doesn't sing in the same way we do. No matter how complex the imitation, it is still imitation. Or maybe I can put it another way: The machine can only imitate the outcome of our thinking. It types out responses which are similar to the responses we humans type out. But the machine can't imitate the thought behind it.

PHIL: Well, we seem to be regressing at a rapid rate. You are saying again it is not just a matter of what machines do—play chess, for example—it is a matter of how they do it. You recall, I hope, that we tried to deal with this problem before. We pointed out how difficult it is to explain notions like "the thinking behind" the performance, unless such thinking was something like typing or talking to oneself—and why shouldn't a machine be able to do this? And just how do human beings think? How much do we know about this? Do psychologists agree on it? There are, after all, all kinds of theories about how humans think. Do you know enough about human thinking to make your argument stick?

STU: I still think thinking machines have to do more than play the imitation game successfully. After all, the imitation game, no matter how complex, is still only a single game, isn't it?

PHIL: Not really—it is the *game of games*. Any game can be considered part of the imitation game. You can ask B to play checkers, twenty questions, even go-to-the-head-of-the-class.

STU: But there is more to thinking than playing those conversational games.

PHIL: What?

STU: Thinking is always to some purpose. We don't just think. We think *in order to* . . .

PHIL: You are asking whether machines can have purposes, ends, intentions, and so forth?

STU: That's right. Maybe they can play chess, but they cannot be said to think unless they are playing to some purpose, to win or to have fun or for some other human purpose.

PHIL: I don't want to bore or exasperate you, but I will adopt my regular strategy. How do you know you have purposes? Isn't it just sometimes that you tell yourself "my goal is this," "here's what I want," "I sure would enjoy a good game of chess"? Sometimes, it's a matter of your having enjoyed certain activities in the past; and so, other things being equal, you want to do those things again.

STU: I can accept something like your account. But how can you make sense of a machine enjoying something? It can "say" it enjoyed something, all right, but it can't really enjoy anything. It can't because it has no feelings. I probably should have hit you with this point earlier.

PHIL: Tell me what feelings you had the last time you played a good game of chess—or tennis, for that matter. Where exactly were your feelings of enjoyment—in the stomach, the head, the elbows? I think we make too much of feelings. Of course we do have feelings, ticklish sensations, pains, feelings of warmth, comfort—but our thinking doesn't seem to involve these kinds of feelings in any intimate or essential way. And then there's the old problem about how you can know that other people have feelings. Surely you admit to knowing or at least to believing on good grounds that they have feelings. Don't you infer the feelings on the basis of the way the people behave? If you adopt this behaviorist position with respect to other people, why not accept behaviorism with respect to machines? I hope you're not just an antimachine bigot!

STU: Behaviorism only seems to make sense with respect to people. If I'm not sure I'm dealing with people, then I cannot be sure I'm dealing with behavior, people's behavior. What worries me is that I can employ behaviorist criteria only if I already know who is a human being—or at least a human being candidate—and who is the machine. So I would have to have some way of telling independently of the feelings-behaviorist argument to distinguish humans from machines.

PHIL: I was about to bring this up myself . . .

STU: Wait, I haven't given up yet. What about *this* argument? One—only living things can have feelings. Two—a computer is not a living thing. Three—therefore, a computer cannot have feelings. Therefore, a computer is not a human being.

PHIL: There are a number of things I can say about this. First, I am always impressed with the appeal to *arguments*. But why should I accept premise one of the argument? The notion *living thing* is not sufficiently clear. Where do we draw the line between the living and the nonliving? I mean, for example, are viruses alive? Is it clear that a nonliving thing can't have feelings? Or perhaps computers can be said to be living things according to some reasonable definition of *living thing*.

STU: You must be kidding. If a machine is a living thing, then I give up. Machines are clear examples of nonliving things. This is true no matter how vague the concept *living thing* is.

PHIL: Even if I grant you this, you still haven't shown that nonliving things can't think. In general, I don't think you've made much progress.

STU: I can see that you are feeling confident, and that's OK with me. And I will admit that I haven't gotten very far, but after all I am a mere student—of mathematics, it is true, but still a student. You, on the other hand, are a professor of philosophy. It hasn't really been a fair fight. I know a mathematics professor who I am sure could deal with you on more even terms. I've discussed this mind/machine question with him and I can assure you that he is no friend of mechanism. In fact, he has told me on several occasions that he has a mathematical refutation of mechanism. Would you be willing to meet with him and me sometime tomorrow to see if you can refute his refutation, or do you argue only with students?

PHIL: As you should know, we philosophers will pursue truth wherever that pursuit takes us—even to a professor of mathematics. By all means bring him with you.

The Second Day

MATT: Stu here tells me he could use some help, so here I am. I know you philosophers can be pretty rough. And I would even bet that there would be many of your own kind who would disagree with you. I am sure that the argument I'm about to present is not as simple as others you have discussed. My argument requires among other things an understanding of a mathematical-logical result known as *Gödel's theorem,* one of the great scientific discoveries of the twentieth century. This is not merely a great scientific discovery, but also a great philosophical discovery, because this theorem, suitably explained and interpreted, proves once and for all that man is not a machine and that machines do not think. I hear you know something about Turing machines and formal mathematical systems, so you shouldn't have too much difficulty following the argument.

PHIL: I'm all ears.

MATT: We do seem to have an intuitive idea of machine. Our English term "machine" comes from the Greek term for apparatus or contrivance. You have apparently given examples of the kind of machine we are discussing, e.g., *Fischkov.* But what is the essence of a machine? Surely not that it have gears, vacuum tubes, transistors, or microchips. In order to apply Gödel's mathematical-logical result to the man/machine problem, we need some way to link our intuitive talk about machines with Gödel's talk about formal systems or theories. We require some mathematical or logical property to serve as deputy for our intuitive commonsense or philosophical notion of *mechanical.* In other words, we need a bridge principle. Note that the bridge principle must have one foot in mathematical logic and the other foot outside in philosophy or psychology. Fortunately, there is such a principle available. It is not a mathematical-logical theorem but rather a thesis—a hypothesis, even; an explication of an intuitive notion in mathematical terms. This thesis is known as *Church's thesis.* Before I present it to you, I want to sharpen up our intuitive notion of *machine.* We need to do this so we can appreciate exactly what Church's thesis says.

First of all I distinguish between physical devices and mechanical devices. Not all physical devices are mechanical, and mechanical devices need not be physical. Machines must have discrete states, and their operations must be describable in discrete terms. Roughly speaking, machines are digital, or discrete-state, computers. We can thus suppose that the behavior of any machine can be described by the input and by the sequence of its states. Church's thesis, our bridge principle, can be expressed as follows: *What can be calculated by a machine is computable.*[2] *We now need to explain computable. Here we can simply use computable to mean computable by a Turing machine. There are many equivalent notions of computable, one of which is representability in a formal system. I will be switching back and forth between "computable by a Turing machine" and the formal-system interpretation of computable. A formal system can best be looked at as a set of instructions to a moron (you'll pardon the grossly insensitive expression). Strings of signs can be scanned, and some can be identified as axioms and others as rules given also recognized only on the basis of shape which would allow theorems to be generated from the axioms. Nothing needs to be understood;* the only requirement is that shapes and forms be recognizable. Now we are ready to appreciate the force of Church's thesis and to see how it, in conjunction with Gödel's theorem, provides us with a neat refutation of mechanism.

Given Church's thesis, it can be seen that all machines are equivalent to Turing machines or formal systems. As you remember, I hope, these Turing machines or idealized machines have a finite number of internal configurations. Each of these configurations represents a state of the machine. In each of these states the machine scans a tape on which certain symbols appear. The tape is divided into discrete units on each of which a symbol from a determinate alphabet may be printed. The machine can scan one square at a time and has a printing and erasing device. A Turing machine can be described completely by a *machine table* which shows how the machine operates from step-to-step. Thanks to Church's and closely related theses I will not go into, *we can thus talk interchangeably about machines, Turing machines, and formal systems.* I've certainly been talking enough. Are you still there?

PHIL: I'm here, and I think I've followed most of what you have said, albeit I do not have a clear idea of where you are going with all of this. I do agree that we need a good definition

2. *What can be calculated by a machine* is our rendering of Church's expression effectively calculable.

of *machine*, but Church's thesis, which seems so obvious to you, hasn't quite convinced me. It does seem to capture what is mechanical about machines. (Isn't there an *analog/digital* distinction which may be relevant here?) Perhaps I need to think a bit more about it. I don't see that you have really argued for it. Didn't you mention Gödel's theorem a while back? Where will *it* fit into your argument against mechanism?

MATT: I was just getting to that. Gödel, or maybe it was Gödel and Church himself, showed—that is, proved—that all formal systems have certain limitations. (Remember that if formal systems have limitations, so do the machines which correspond to them.) Take a formal system for arithmetic, one that can express *plus* and *times*. If this formal system contains *all* the truths of this arithmetic as logical consequences of the axioms of the system, then the system is said to be *complete*, an important concept. There is one way to guarantee that a system is complete. Can you see how?

PHIL: I can. But feel free to answer the question for Stu's sake.

MATT: By making the system inconsistent: all sentences of arithmetic will follow from an inconsistent set of sentences. That's why it is so important to avoid contradictions. Any old thing follows from them. We are interested in *complete* and *consistent* formal systems. By the way, suppose there is even one sentence of arithmetic that is not a theorem (deducible) in the formal system; what would follow?

PHIL: Given what you said before, even one sentence that is not deducible would mean that the system is *consistent*. By the way, can you prove that anything follows from a contradiction? Could you demonstrate this to a logically unsophisticated person like Stu?

MATT: Sure. What would you like me to deduce? Choose any old thing.

PHIL: OK, prove to us that 2 + 2 = 5.

MATT: Let me begin by writing down the inconsistent or

contradictory sentences. Let me call them *P* and *not-P*. We can call these the premises of the argument. Let's call 2 + 2 = 5 by the letter *Q*. I will now proceed to deduce *Q* from *P* and *not-P*. First I can write down *P*. The justification is that it is a premise. Next I write down *P* or *Q*. *P* or *Q* follows from *P*. If a sentence is true, then the sentence with any *sentence* attached with *or* will also be true. If it is true that *Today is Thursday*, then *Today is Thursday or The moon is made of green cheese* is also true.

PHIL: I think I see that.

MATT: Now I write down *not-P*. After all, it too is a premise. But if *P* or *Q* is true and *not-P* is true, then obviously *Q* has to be true. So you see from a contradiction I have deduced that 2 + 2 = 5. You can see why mathematically and logically sophisticated people hate contradictions. Contradictions are the *spoilers* of rational thinking.

PHIL: OK, I see why we want systems which are both consistent and complete. Can't we have them?

MATT: No, not always. Gödel showed that a formal system which includes the arithmetic of plus and times must be either inconsistent or incomplete—or equivalently, that if the system is consistent, then it is incomplete. This is Gödel's conclusion. Let's see how he got there.

Consider a formal axiomatic system for arithmetic. Such a system aims at systematizing the truths of arithmetic. What is sought is a system which is both complete—all the truths are theorems (logical consequences of the axiom, and the axioms are, of course, logical consequences of themselves)—and consistent (there must be at least one arithmetical sentence that is not a theorem, for if the system were inconsistent, all arithmetical sentences would be theorems, true and false ones alike). The language for our arithmetical system will contain symbols like '1,' '13,' '+,' '=' as well as logical symbols. Most sentences will be of the form "1 + 1 = 2," or "8 × 3 = 24." A proof is simply a sequence of these sentences beginning with axioms and ending with a logical consequence of these axioms. Remember that what is or is not a proof is simply a mechanical matter, something our "moron" or Turing machine can handle. It is all a matter of having the right shape, form, or configuration. In the arithmetical system we talk about numbers and numerical relationships. What Gödel has shown is that there is a way of using the arithmetical sentences of the system to talk not only about numbers but also about the sentences of the systems. Arithmetical sentences can be so coded that they can be given an interpretation according to which they say something about themselves. The details of Gödel's technique, called Gödel numbering, need not concern us, but I believe I can give you a working idea of the technique. We list the vocabulary employed in the system and assign a numeral to each symbol. Combinations of symbols, especially sentences, will possess numerals resulting from the combination of their constituent symbols. Each sentence then gets its unique Gödel number through its unique Gödel numeral. Properties of sentences are represented by arithmetical properties; for example, "is an axiom," "is a theorem," will be represented by arithmetical properties. Our code allows us to say things such as that $7 \times 6 = 42$ is a theorem exclusively within the language of arithmetic. We can put things somewhat less vaguely. Let us call the formal system of Arithmetic Σ. To each formula of Σ, sentences included, a unique numeral and number is assigned. This procedure allows us to encode logical derivations and even provides us with an encoded version of the proof relation. It will simply be some complicated arithmetical *functor* (or arithmetical *function* if we switch from numeral talk to number talk). In other words if [m], where the bracketed letters are numbers or variables for numbers, bears the arithmetical version of the proof relation to [n] (if [m] is a *proof* of [n]), then the sentence encoded by [n] can be said to be a theorem of Σ. So within Σ, through encoding, we can speak of *theoremhood* and *non-theoremhood*. This talk about theoremhood and so forth is said to be grammatical, syntactical, metalinguistic, metamathematical talk.

What Gödel accomplished was the arithmetization of the syntax of arithmetic. Gödel showed that we could use mathematics to talk about mathematics, that we could use mathematics to do metamathematics. Among the sentences we can express in our arithmetical code is the sentence *S is not a theorem* where S is itself the sentence S *is not a theorem.* S thus says of itself that it is not a theorem. There is a sentence of our arithmetical system which under the coding says that it itself is not a theorem. What Gödel concluded was that because this arithmetical sentence, call it S, says of itself that it is not a theorem, that S must be *undecidable* for the arithmetical system in question if the system is consistent. For if the system contained S, it would follow that S is a theorem, but S says (under the coding) that S is not a theorem. We would have S both a theorem because the system contained it and not a theorem because S says that it is not a theorem. Thus S is and is not a theorem. Well, if S is not a theorem, then perhaps *not-S,* the sentence which says S is a *theorem,* is a theorem. But if *not-S* is a theorem, then S is a theorem, but S is S *is not a theorem.* So we have again a contradiction: S *is a theorem,* S *is not a theorem.* S is thus an undecidable arithmetical sentence for our system. S is accordingly said to be an *undecidable sentence.* Any formal axiomatic system for arithmetic, including plus and times, will have an undecidable sentence. What we have here is thus a limitation of formal systems of a certain wide-ranging kind: if they are consistent, then they are incomplete. This is Gödel's famous incompleteness result. It applies to formal systems, or to Turing machines—and if we accept Church's thesis to the effect that a machine is simply a realization of a formal system or Turing machine, then Gödel has demonstrated a limitation of machines in general or at least of any modest machine which can do arithmetic. Given this result I suppose you can see what the next step in the argument will be.

PHIL: I can see where you are going, but I really would like some time to review the Gödel argument. We philosophers don't often see arguments laid out this way. Give me some time to do some thinking and perhaps even some reading. Then I'll be more than happy to have you put the finishing touches on your argument. Gödel's theorem as a refutation of mechanism—the mind boggles.

The Third Day

PHIL: I'm ready to have you put the cap on your "refutation" of mechanism (man = machine). I'm going to have some questions for you, though.

MATT: OK. Gödel proved that formal systems rich enough to contain the arithmetic of plus and times are either inconsistent or incomplete. If they are consistent, they are incomplete; that is, there are some true sentences which are not provable in the system. Turing machines mimicking these formal systems will exhibit a parallel limitation; they will be unable to crank out or print out all the truths of arithmetic. It is the sentence S, where *S = S is not provable*—the Gödel sentence—which machines cannot decide on that represents what one author has called the "Achilles Heel of Mechanism." We differ from the machines; we are superior in at least one respect: we can identify some truths that machines cannot. In fact, we know that the Gödel sentence is true. Let me restate this: Any mechanical simulation of the mind must include a machine that can generate the truths of arithmetic. After all, arithmetic is something the human mind has mastered. There is one respect in which the simulation of mind must fail: the arithmetic component will not be able to exhibit the truth of some statement, which we can. This shows that a mechanical simulation of the mind is impossible; the mind is not a machine. So much, too, for *Fischkov III!* An English *philosopher* named Lucas came up with this argument, but I am proud as a *mathematician* to have adopted it.

PHIL: It looks to me as if you have something like an imitation-game argument to the effect that the interrogator will be able to distinguish the man from the machine by asking questions of a metamathematical nature. If the interrogator knew his Gödel and his Church, the human being could emerge victorious over the machine. My Turing machine argument has come back to haunt me.

MATT: I suppose you can look at my argument that way if you want.

PHIL: The machine is asked: Could you prove S, the Gödel sentence? It answers, I can't prove S and I can't prove *not-S*. S is an undecidable sentence for me. This S, of course, is an actual arithmetical sentence. Coded, it says that S is not provable. When a human responds to the same question, the answer is: "Though the sentence is unprovable in the system, I can see that it is true." (Machines "say" sentences are true by cranking them out, formal systems by including the sentences as theorems.) I will grant you the machine can't decide whether S is true or not. What makes you so sure the human being can?

MATT: It's not that we can see its truth as an arithmetical sentence. After all, the machine is likely to be better at arithmetic than we are. It is the coded interpretation; it is S as a syntactical, metamathematical sentence that enables us to recognize its truth. We know that *S is not a theorem*, where S = *S is not a theorem*, because if S were false, the system would be inconsistent; but we know the system is consistent, so S has to be true. ". . . any rational being could follow Gödel's argument, and convince herself that the Gödelian formula, although unprovable in the given system, was nonetheless in fact, for that very reason, true."[3]

PHIL: I don't see why the machine itself can't follow Gödel's argument. The machine participating in the imitation game is after all more than an arithmetic-machine; there is nothing in Gödel's proof that a machine cannot handle.

MATT: You miss the point. The arithmetic machine component has its Gödel sentence, but the more comprehensive machine that includes the arithmetical component has its own Gödel sentence. It is this sentence which the comprehensive machine

3. J. R. Lucas, "Minds, Machines and Gödel," in A. R. Anderson, ed., *Minds and Machines*, p. 47.

cannot handle, but we can. You see, no machine, no matter how comprehensive, will be able to avoid a Gödel sentence; hence, it will be unable to defend its own consistency—but we humans can see that the machine is consistent.

PHIL: But how can you be so sure that the more comprehensive system is consistent and thus that its S is true—only by appealing to the consistency of the arithmetical system which encodes even the more comprehensive system? And why couldn't the machine do something analogous? After all, the machine can prove that *if* M is consistent, then S. (S is not provable.) You still have to show the consistency of M, something I will grant you, M cannot demonstrate.

MATT: You're getting pretty good at these arguments. What I can show is that M is consistent because I, including my arithmetical component, am consistent, and M is supposed to represent me.

PHIL: OK, show me how you can defend your own consistency. I can see that you might have to *assume* your consistency. But I can't see how you can *demonstrate it*.

MATT: Well, let me remind you that Gödel's second theorem showed that a machine cannot prove its own consistency, but it

> seems to be both proper and reasonable for a mind to assert its own consistency: proper, because although machines, as we might have expected, are unable to reflect fully on their own performance and powers, yet to be able to be self-conscious in this way is just what we expect of minds: and reasonable, for the reasons with fairness given. Not only can we say simply that we *know* we are consistent, apart from our mistakes, but we must in any case *assume* that we are, if thought is to be possible at all. Moreover, we are selective: we will not, as inconsistent machines would, say anything and everything whatsoever; and finally we can, in a sense, *decide* to be consistent, in the sense that we can resolve not to tolerate inconsistencies in our thinking and speaking, and to eliminate them, if

> ever they should appear, by withdrawing and can-
> celing one limb of the contradiction.[4]

PHIL: Things get "curiouser and curiouser." You begin with
an argument based on Gödel's theorem and Church's thesis
and ultimately you rest your case on what seem to me to be
vague and metaphysical claims about human self-consciousness and the consistency of the human mind. I'm not
even sure we can make good sense of talk about human
beings being consistent or inconsistent. And if we can, I
have an interesting argument up my sleeve. I think you
should take another look at the strategy of your argument.
You tried to use Gödel's first theorem to refute mechanism;
but then you noted the consistency feature of the first
theorem. You had to show that though the machine could
not handle the consistency problem (Gödel's second theorem), a human being could. You argued that the system was
consistent because human minds are consistent; and human
minds can establish their consistency because they are by
their very nature self-conscious.

MATT: Let me stop you here. Don't you see, this is the heart of
my argument. Machines are *inanimate* objects, and they con-
sequently cannot recognize their own consistency.

PHIL: And what exactly is an *inanimate* object—or *animate,* for
that matter—and how do you get from *animate* to self-conscious? Things seem to be going from bad to worse. I thought
you were going to use a mathematical argument.

MATT: I admit that my argument does seem to be a matter more
of conceptual analysis than mathematical demonstration. The
key is the concept of (*self-*)*consciousness.* You have to see, for
instance, that

> the concept of conscious being is, implicitly, realized
> to be different from that of an unconscious object. In
> saying that a conscious being knows something, we
> are saying not only that he knows it, but that he

4. Ibid., p. 56.

knows that he knows it, and that he knows that he
knows that he knows it, and so on, as long as we care
to pose the question; there is, we recognize, an infin-
ity here, but it is not an infinite regress in the bad
sense, for it is the questions that peter out, as being
pointless, rather than the answers.[5]

PHIL: Your retreat to conceptual analysis appears to me a total
defeat, I'm afraid. Why did you need Gödel in the first place?
Was it somehow the special nature of Gödel sentences as
self-referring?

MATT: You have hit the nail right on the head. We humans can
manage the self-reflection necessary to answer the Gödel
questions, but a machine is helpless with Gödel sentences.

PHIL: Maybe you're smarter than I am, but I fail to see that
self-reference is an *inherent* property of Gödel sentences. Isn't
self-reference simply due to the particular coding? The arithmetical statement S = itself need not involve any self-reference
at all. Anyway, would you want your whole intricate argument, your "refutation" of mechanism, to rest on this point?

MATT: I think I'll take the Fifth Amendment on that one. I was
so sure of this argument until our discussion that now I feel
somewhat numbed. You philosophers have a well-deserved
reputation for confusing people.

PHIL: But don't you think that for all your confusion you are
now better off? Now, at least, you know that you did not
know. I've got a few other questions to ask you about your
argument. But before I ask them, I've been doing some home-
work, and I have a semioriginal counterargument to perplex
you further.

   The original argument attempted to show that all machines had to be either *inconsistent* or *incomplete*. This was the
limitation on machines that made us humans superior. We
were complete without being inconsistent. But aren't we
speakers of English really even in worse shape than machines? Because machines have the Gödel limitation, they

5. Ibid., p. 57.

cannot encode the ordinary English notion of truth (they are stuck with provability); the assumption that arithmetic could completely encode English and the notion of truth, an assumption Gödel did not make, has to be false. The nearest it can come, as we have seen, is *provability*. Machines assert truths by proving theorems. We can (justifiably) assert truths without proving anything. All we require is some kind of justification. *Theoremhood* is the machine approximation closest to *truth*. Any assumption that the arithmetical coding of English could be expressively complete is, as we indicated above, in error. But this looks simply like another way of showing our superiority over arithmetic and its machine realizations. *We* can distinguish truth from theoremhood (provability), but machines cannot. The Gödel sentence, you remember, was a sentence the machine couldn't prove, yet we were able to "see" its truth. If it weren't true, arithmetic and that part of our English which includes arithmetic and thus our English would be inconsistent, and this we "know" or "see" is not the case. But isn't it an advantage that the machine cannot express truth the way we can in English? Why? Because we unfortunately could come up with what appears to be a perfectly good English sentence that says of itself *not* that it isn't provable but that it isn't true; e.g., *S is not true*, where "S" names *S is not true* ["S" is an abbreviation for "S" is not true"]. Since we called the other sentence (the provability sentence) after Gödel, let's call this new sentence after the great Polish logician and developer of the *semantic theory of truth*, Alfred Tarski: the *Tarski sentence*. English unlike arithmetic contains Tarski sentences. But any language which contains a Tarski sentence must be inconsistent, for Tarski sentences are true if and only if they are false (and false if and only if they are true). So English is inconsistent, so English speakers (French or Spanish speakers too, for that matter) are inconsistent. But machine arithmetic speakers are not necessarily inconsistent; Gödel showed that they are merely either inconsistent or incomplete; and isn't it better to be *either* inconsistent or incomplete than to be inconsistent? Isn't, for instance, incompleteness a lesser vice or weakness? So doesn't the Gödel-Church-Lucas argument really wind up proving our inferiority to robots rather than our superiority over them?

MATT: Please have mercy and let me go home and take a few Advils. When my head clears I'll return for some more punishment. Maybe then I'll be able to turn the tables on you. It makes for a nice dream, anyway.

Four Hours Later

MATT: I'm back and I feel better. My confidence has returned. I'll even let you begin!

PHIL: I want to talk a bit more about Church's thesis, the thesis which, roughly speaking, identifies a machine as some realization of a formal system or a Turing machine. I'm not so sure we should accept this definition; after all, it is a definition or explication and not a mathematical or logical result. Of course, without Church's thesis your entire argument (and my rejoinder) would collapse at the beginning, because you could not argue from the limitations of formal systems (from Gödel's result) to limitations about machines in general.

MATT: But almost everybody accepts Church's thesis.

PHIL: Is that supposed to be an argument?

MATT: Seriously, Church's thesis provides us with a precise explication of the intuitive concept, *mechanical procedure*. It explicates mechanical procedure in terms of mathematical notions like formal systems and Turing machines. Furthermore, the fact that the different explications of mechanical procedure—that is, in terms of formal systems and Turing machines turning out to be equivalent—provides further indirect confirmation of Church's thesis. (In other words, Church's thesis [recursiveness], Turing's thesis [Turing machine], and the Kleene-Post thesis [formal systems] turn out to be equivalent.) I admit though that one could never *prove* that an intuitive notion like mechanical procedure was equivalent to a precise mathematical expression in terms of

Turing machines or formal systems. If you don't find all this persuasive, I challenge you to come up with some better explication, or at least some competitor to Church's thesis. You haven't even yet given me some reason for doubting Church's thesis. Do you think machines can do more than Church's thesis says they can?

PHIL: Well, first I simply wanted to remind you that your entire argument, bad as it was, rests firmly on the acceptance of Church's thesis. I will grant you that the acceptance of Church's thesis does permit us to talk about machines in a precise way. I appreciate the increase in clarity, but there is more required of good explication than that the explicating expression (*explicans*) be clear or precise; it must also adequately capture the intuitive notion. I am still troubled, for instance, with analog/digital distinction . . .

MATT: You haven't yet provided me with any clear alternative to Church's thesis. It seems to me that unless you can do this, we are severely limited in our ability to deal with the mind/machine problem. Church's thesis gives us a way of understanding *machine*, and a mathematically elegant way at that.

PHIL: Maybe there is some alternative mathematically elegant way of representing machines, and maybe there is no such mathematically elegant explication at all. After all, we need not necessarily despair of explicating this in an elegant way. Clarity and precision do not necessarily mean mathematical clarity and precision.

MATT: Well, I would think twice before giving up the high road of mathematics. Remember, you weren't doing all that well, were you, before we examined my mathematical "refutation" of mechanism?

PHIL: Though I'm not prepared to accept Church's thesis without further argument, I do not, of course, think this is the weakest part of your argument. That honor has to go to your vague talk of consciousness, self-consciousness, and human consistency.[6] These are certainly advantages to accepting Church's thesis. As you pointed out, it does give us a precise way to talk about machines. Only *I believe* one can successfully argue that Church's thesis applies to us, too. Human beings can be seen as realizations of Turing machines (or, of course, realizations of formal systems). We have to remember that Turing machines are mathematical rather than physical objects. If a machine can perform some act, that act can be represented as an act of a Turing machine.

MATT: Of course I grant you the last point. In fact, as you may remember, I employed the notion of a Turing machine to help me make my case against mechanism.

PHIL: Now I want to turn the tables a bit and argue that you and I are TMs (Turing machines), or, more accurately, flesh and blood realizations of TMs. We have talked an awful lot about machines, and much less about human beings. It has been almost as if we assumed we had a clear explication of *human being*, as if we had something like Church's thesis for the human being. What is a *human being*? We have the famous *rational animal* answer; but these terms, of course, themselves require explanation. Structurally, man has been said to have a mind and a body, the mind being responsible for our thinking and consciousness. Of course, man also has a brain as part of his body. As for the precise nature of the relationships between mind and body, mind and brain, mental state and physical state, there are many answers, but there is no consensus on some single defensible answer. I don't think we will ever resolve the mind/machine problem or the "Is man a machine?" problem unless we develop better answers to these questions.

MATT: I've never found what you philosophers call the mind/body problem to be all that difficult. It's just a matter of paying attention to some obvious facts and the meaning of

6. The best attempt I know of at making sense of Lucas's appeal to self-consciousness and the like is in D. Hofstadter, *Metamagical Themas*, *"On the Seeming Paradox of Mechanizing Creativity."*

identity—a term, by the way, with which we mathematicians are quite familiar. Mental states could not be identical to physical states because we are directly aware of many of our own mental states and we do not infer or obtain this knowledge from observation or from our own behavior or from observation of our brain. So mental states have at least one property physical states do not; hence mental states are not identical to physical states. Anyway, these mind/body problems just don't arise for machines. This is because machines don't have mental states. But why don't you go on with our argument? There is an argument coming up, I take it.

PHIL: Of course! I want to argue that the same difficult and, at least for me, unanswered questions which I raised above can also be raised for Turing machines.[7] For instance, the mind/body problem has a TM analog. In other words, those problems usually taken to be distinctive of human beings are not distinctive at all. And if this is the case, there is no reason not to classify human beings and TMs together.

MATT: What you have in mind—excuse me—seems to be an unpromising and very roundabout argument. But I'll let you pursue your analogy further.

PHIL: A TM is identical to its program, and its program or instruction table is simply a sequence of instructions specifying in each case what to do given a certain input; for instance, erase the input symbol, print a symbol, move to left, and enter the next state (follow the next set of instructions). When a TM is following a certain set of instructions such as α, we can say that it is in state α. Given input and state, we can predict what the TM will do. These states of the TM we can call *logical* or *program* states—and they correspond to our mental states.

   Philosophers have long raised questions about our knowledge of mental states. Some of these states seem to be states we can be in without our knowing that we are in them. We can, for instance, be jealous without knowing it. How do we

7. The argument coming up is Hilary Putnam's. See "Minds and Machines" in A. R. Anderson's *Minds and Machines*.

know when we are jealous? We sometimes simply observe our own behavior. For a TM to be jealous, its mental state would have to be realized or embodied in a suitable way, with perceiving or sensing devices. Some of our mental states, however, are different. For us to be in these states is to know that we are having a certain experience. "How do you know you have a headache? I know because I have a headache." The TM can mimic this by being programmed to print that it is in a certain state when and only when it is in that state. (This is the way it has been programmed, much as we have been programmed to say "ouch" when we are in pain.) With this second kind of mental state, we do not need to know anything of our bodily state to know we are in the state. In connection with the TM's analogous *logical or program states*, there also need be no knowledge of bodily or embodiment states. For bodily states, both man and TM need special sensor or observational devices. For both man and machine, laws relating mental (logical) and bodily or brain states must be based on experience. Any claim for identity of a logical state and physical state—for instance, whenever I am in state 236, flipflops 73 and 227 are on—requires a special interpretation of *identity*; that is, we require the *is* of theoretical identification: for example, the *is* in *light is electromagnetic radiation*, or *water is* H_2O. The important thing to note is that the mind/body (brain) identification problem has an exactly analogous problem for TMs (the problem of identifying logical and embodiment states). Even another important philosophical problem—the problem of other minds, the problem of how we can know the thoughts or mental states of others even though we cannot "get inside" other people's minds, feel their feelings, think their thoughts, and so forth—has a TM analog. Clearly, this "knowledge" is a matter of inference from the behavior, including the verbal behavior, of others. The other-minds problem for TMs is the problem of identifying the logical states of other TMs. For us, for other TMs, this too has to be a matter of inference.

MATT: OK, I agree that those TM problems are similar to many traditional problems about the nature of man and human knowledge. But all this is analogy, similarity; what can it possibly show? Surely not that man is a machine, an embodied TM. At most you have shown that there are a number of respects in which man and TMs are similar. How can this fancy philosophical argument be used to support mechanism?

PHIL: For one thing, my argument shows that man is not so special; that is, TMs share all those problems with humans. If you are going to answer the mind/body problem by stating that the mind is something different from the body, you will have to say that a TM's logical states are distinct from its structural or embodied states. If your mind/body argument were to lead you, in the spirit of generosity, to give human beings souls, you would by parallel reasoning be obliged to give souls to TMs. My argument is rather subtle and indirect. By stressing likenesses between humans and TMs, I am showing you how difficult it will be to come up with arguments against the man=machine thesis. I claim that when you come up with an argument that has man exhibit some "special" property, I will be able to come up with a parallel argument showing you that TMs, too, exhibit that "special" property. In fact, this has been my general strategy all along.

MATT: Well, it still seems to me that what you've presented is more like a promise than an argument. And, of course, if my "mathematical" argument from the limitations of formal systems (the Lucas argument) is a good one, then you will not be able to make good on your promise. There will be at least one area where there is something "special" (seeing the truth of Gödel sentences) which distinguishes us from machines.

PHIL: *If* your argument is a good one! That "if" is a big little word, since we saw that your argument had several serious shortcomings. But this is old ground by now.

MATT: I still believe there is something in my argument—a human being cannot be represented by some formal system. We can handle symbols in a way formal systems cannot. What I need to do is clarify this idea in a way that precludes your objection to my previous attempt. Maybe I relied too heavily on Gödel's theorem. Perhaps there is some more general argument. If I can't find one, I'll give up this line of thought altogether and beat you with some other less "mathematical" argument.

PHIL: Why don't we take a break. I'll treat you and Stu to a Big Mac and then we'll take another shot at it.

After Lunch

MATT: Here I am, back for more punishment.

PHIL: Don't you think you've been giving as good as you've been getting?

MATT: I'm not sure, but maybe my Big Mac brought me new intellectual vigor. Human thinking, it seems to me, is not formal, not finite and definite. Human thinking is intuitive, informal, and self-conscious. We can see things at a glance, grasp wholes. No machine can ever fully reflect on itself. Such reflection would require adding components indefinitely.

PHIL: So far it seems to me you are simply restating some of your previous claims.

MATT: OK, try this out. Formal systems abstract from questions of meaning. They are concerned only with symbol forms or with marks on paper. Any formal system, a system of marks on paper, is susceptible to more than one interpretation. Without a mind to provide a single intended meaning, machines are necessarily incomplete. Machines as realizations of formal systems can never be properly said to *understand* anything. One writer—a scientist and philosopher, by the way—put the matter this way:

> . . . a formalized deductive system is an instrument which requires for its logical completion a mind using the instrument in a manner not fully determined by the instrument; while the mind of the person using the instrument requires no such logical completion . . . Herein lies the difference between mind and machine.[8]

8. Michael Polanyi, "Note on the Hypothesis of Cybernetics," *The British Journal for the Philosophy of Science 2*, 1951, p. 314.

And I've even come up with a knockdown argument against your position. I am going to introduce you to Robo-Traffic-Cop.

Robo-Traffic-Cop, built in Toledo and programmed at Cal Tech, stands on a platform in the center of Times Square in midtown Manhattan. Cars drive by . . . slow down traffic, if that is possible in midtown Manhattan, and request directions, e.g., how do I get to Grant's Tomb? Robo-Traffic-Cop rattles off the right directions, sometimes even pointing the drivers in the right way. Sometimes he admits he doesn't know or adds, "That's a tough one." He even sometimes comments on the weather. And Robo-Traffic-Cop is one good-looking cop: 6'2", red hair, sometimes nicknamed "Red" or "O'Hara." Well, I think I've said enough for you to see how silly your own imitation game is as a strategy for determining human intelligence. Surely you don't believe that Robo-Traffic-Cop really understands anything said to him or said by him; yet his behavior is perfectly appropriate. According to John Searle—a philosopher both Stu and I think highly of—Robo-Traffic-Cop doesn't understand anything because he lacks intentionality, "that feature of certain mental states by which they are directed at or about objects and states of affairs in the world."[9]

PHIL: You've come up with something different, but whether it's better or not . . . To make your point, you require some theory or account of meaning. How do human beings understand? Can you answer that question? If not, how can you toss brickbats at the machine? The whole question of meaning, of semantics, seems rather murky. If we could provide meaning rules for a language—and that's what dictionaries are supposed to do, after all—I don't see why we couldn't add these to the program of the computer. It would be like adding a dictionary to the program. Of course I'll admit that mastery of the dictionary is not itself understanding the language. You could pick up a Rumanian-Rumanian dictionary at your local

9. See John Searle, "Minds, Brains, and Programs" (The Chinese room argument), in Hofstadter and Dennett.

esoteric bookstore and learn all the equivalences. But unless you could understand some of the terms through a direct tie to experience, independent of the dictionary, you could not be said to *understand*. In a sense, we would know what each Rumanian word meant, but we couldn't get from any Rumanian word to the world. So there must be a way to break out of the circle of dictionary definitions to some other kind of explanation of meaning which would tie word with world. Why shouldn't a TM, or rather an embodied (incorporated) TM, learn to say "cat" when a cat is present? And this seems to be a feature of Robo-Traffic-Cop. If we call these rules ostensive (exhibiting, pointing out) rules, then ostensive rules plus a dictionary would provide our TM with sufficient semantic power to deal with your objection. It is only if you treat meanings as entities of some special sort, and the grasping of meanings as some mysterious process, that you cause the machine any difficulty. But obscurity is too high a price to pay for winning an argument.

And recently some philosopher friends of mine have explained how certain features of program software and the like *could be* crucial factors in explicating understanding. You thought it was so obvious that Robo-Traffic-Cop lacked understanding, because you no doubt had a rather simpleminded idea of its program—a straightforward set of rules for transforming symbols. No doubt also you think no matter how complicated such a program, no matter how many levels it has, it remains formal, or syntactical, and this is not the kind of thing that can contribute to understanding or any other mental property. But how can you be so certain that "intermediate level software concepts" will not make a difference?[10]

MATT: I'm sorry, you're still talking magic; you have a theory of *immaculate mentality*. You seem to be having surprisingly little difficulty with my latest challenge; but if dealing with meaning is so easy, why didn't you deal with it earlier?

10. This line taken here is Dennett's in *Consciousness Explained*.

PHIL: First of all, I emphasized that talk about meaning is usually quite murky. Secondly, you have introduced into the conversation something new here with your explicit introduction of meaning and its connection to understanding. A machine doesn't understand arithmetic simply because it is the realization of some formal system for arithmetic, merely because it can crank out arithmetical theorems. Understanding arithmetic requires something more than this. [Grammar or syntax needs to be supplemented with semantics (perhaps even pragmatics, an account of language use and users)]; knowing how strings of marks are put together, knowing what strings are grammatical, does not enable one to know what the grammatical strings mean. A machine should be able to do sums, products, and so forth; to count objects; perhaps even to do problems. Some of these skills go beyond the skills represented by formal systems. But there is no reason to think a machine couldn't accomplish these things also. To count objects it would need sensors; to do problems, it would perhaps need some additional rules for translation and problem solving—unless, of course, there were something about these rules that prevented their representation in a computer program. Unless there is something like a Gödel limitation for these rules, then a machine should be able to handle meaning; to understand, as it were. We shouldn't forget there is *hardware* too.

MATT: Let's talk a bit more about understanding. I repeat, machines may be able to compute, but they are not able to understand.

PHIL: OK, then I challenge you once again to explain to me just what you take *understanding* to be.

MATT: I'm afraid I can't tell you exactly. Understanding is something the mind does. It is a mental act.

PHIL: Not the act in which meanings are grasped? It is going to be difficult to explain this act of mental grasping. Can't you provide us with a definition of understanding with some cash value—a definition that provides us with a way of telling whether "something" understands or not? My point is this: we need not get involved in talk about meanings and interpretations. We need only talk about the formal system and its use; the machine and the way it interacts with objects in the world.

MATT: There goes your behaviorism again. You insist that all mental concepts be interpreted in terms of behavior. What you want is some behavioral test or criterion for understanding. Maybe you'll come up with one, but you will never be able to capture the *essence* of understanding.

PHIL: I don't know about the *essence* of understanding. But it seems to me that if we are going to make sense of a term, we have to look at the way it is used. As Ludwig Wittgenstein put it: Don't ask for the meaning, ask for the use. Under what circumstances do we say, that someone understands something? When does a mathematics student understand, say the Pythagorean theorem [$a^2 + b^2 = c^2$]? It's when he or she is able to relate the theorem to other geometrical statements, to apply the theorem in problem solving....Understanding Newton's theory involves being able to answer questions about the theory's components, to relate the theory to other theories; and of course being able to use the theory to solve problems.

MATT: Machines can compute, they can crank out theorems but they cannot understand. In fact, even if the machine can do the kind of relating you just talked about, I would still deny that it can understand. It is, I am afraid, your behaviorism, your emphasis on performance, that gets in the way again. *Verifiability* is one thing, *truth* is another.

PHIL: Sticks and stones! Tell me what more there is to understanding than the capacity to perform the kinds of things I mentioned. Do you really believe that understanding involves some special experience or sensation? Perhaps you think understanding can be explained in terms of the AHA! phenomenon, a kind of mental illumination (the glowing light bulb of the comic strips).

MATT: You must be reading my mind; but what's wrong with identifying understanding with the AHA! experience? You know, AHA! I see it now! Now I understand!

PHIL: Is the AHA! always present when you understand?

MATT: No, not always.

PHIL: Is the AHA! sometimes present when you don't understand, when you only thought you understood?

MATT: Yes, I suppose so.

PHIL: Then how can you identify understanding with this experience? Furthermore, it's doubtful that there is any single experience that is always present when you have come to understand something. Here too I am following Wittgenstein: you might want to read his *Blue Book* or the *Philosophical Investigations*. But I don't want you to get the idea that my argument consists simply of an appeal to authority. So tell me—just what I have left out in my account of understanding?

MATT: But understanding is basically an informal process, one that can't be spelled out in a set of explicit rules. There is a tacit dimension to much understanding. Think again of the understanding involved in mastery of a language. No formalism can capture this process. As Polanyi said,

> Thus to speak a language is to commit ourselves to the double indeterminacy due to our reliance both on formalism and on our own continued reconsideration of this formalism in its bearing on experience. For just as owing to the ultimately tacit character of all our knowledge, we remain even unable to say all that we know, so also, in view of the tacit character of meaning, we can never quite know what is implied in what we say.[11]

PHIL: I find it difficult to respond to this. I'm not sure I understand you or Polanyi completely. If you can show me that you understand this talk of understanding, then I think I

11. Michael Polanyi, *Personal Knowledge* (London: Routledge & Kegan Paul, 1958).

can show you that a machine can understand in the sense you have introduced. If you cannot show me you understand, what can you expect me to do? There seems to be a touch of mysticism in your comments. You can't expect anyone, man or machine, to "eff" the ineffable.

MATT: Sometimes you sound as if you are speaking for all philosophers; as if behaviorism, or something like it, has become the official philosophy of mind and man. Does your Wittgenstein speak for everybody? You've deflected some of my arguments even before I offered them. You seem especially sure of yourself on this issue of meaning and understanding. I have also noticed that you do not appeal much to the philosophical tradition in presenting your arguments. I've heard little of Plato, Aristotle, Descartes, or Kant.

PHIL: You're right. I certainly haven't dropped many names. Why appeal to authority when the arguments can stand on their own? I could, of course, have more frequently mentioned Wittgenstein and Ryle and a few other contemporary philosophers. By the way, you and Stu have shown yourselves largely to be followers of Descartes, who emphasized the distinction between mind and body. You appear to be sympathetic to what Gilbert Ryle termed the "Ghost in the Machine" theory of mind. Ryle "refutes" this view in his *Concept of Mind*.[12] I believe that the mind/machine problem has only become tantalizing in the present era of sophisticated digital computers, after all; so it's hardly surprising that I stick to contemporary philosophers and philosophy.

MATT: Well, you're the philosopher; but as I see it, you're selling a very old product—*materialism*—and I'm sure that in the philosophical tradition there have been many discussions of materialism. Although I don't make a habit of reading philosophers, at least the professionals, I have read some whom you would no doubt dismiss as pop philosophers— "pop" meaning, I gather, that the general public can under-

12. Gilbert Ryle, *Concept of Mind* (New York: Barnes and Noble, 1949).

stand them, this being a high crime. From one of these philosophers, Mortimer Adler, I learned of the following argument rooted in the work of Aristotle and St. Thomas. From our discussion so far I would even doubt that you are familiar with the argument; it's probably not contemporary enough for you. It aims to show that understanding requires some *immaterial* component, and hence that a materialist conception of man, a conception such as your own, cannot be adequate. Your brand of behaviorism amounts to materialism as I see it, and I believe I can refute materialism.

PHIL: Let's have the argument—but remember, you won't intimidate me with great names like Aristotle, Aquinas, and Adler. And I deny, by the way, that my philosophical behaviorism, my insistence on providing an analysis of mental terms in terms of behavior and machine programs, commits me to materialism. But go on.

MATT: When we understand something—for instance, what it is to be a man—we understand it by means of a concept. Without concepts we could not understand. But concepts are not material things, because all material things are individuals, as are individual men or toothpicks—but the concept of *man* is not identical to any individual; it is a universal thing. Material things could not deal with concepts, but understanding requires this transaction with concepts. Understanding, therefore, requires something more than the brain, since the brain is a material thing. There must be some immaterial part of a man, a mind, an intellect, in order for man to understand. And if thinking requires understanding, machines, which are material things, cannot think. And if human beings are necessarily beings who can think, then *machines cannot be humans*. While this is no mathematical demonstration, it looks pretty good to me.

PHIL: What you have made use of in your argument is a certain psychological or philosophical-psychological theory. This theory attempts to explain how understanding is possible. According to this theory, if Herby understands what it is to be a doorknob, then it is only because he has formed or grasped the concept *doorknob*. Why accept this theoretical claim? All we know is that Herby can respond appropriately to doorknobs and questions about doorknobs, etc. He has learned the appropriate discriminations, just as a pigeon can learn to distinguish red objects from objects of a different color. Do you want to say that pigeons are partly immaterial?

MATT: But there is a difference between perceptual discrimination and intellectual understanding. Unlike the pigeon, we can understand redness or triangularity. We can answer questions about these abstract objects themselves.

PHIL: When you say we can understand redness itself, you seem to mean that we know how to use the term "redness." That this use presupposes an immaterial concept of redness is still open to question. To me it is simply a matter of the appropriate conditioning. The conditioning process is more complex than it needs to be for the pigeon to distinguish red objects, but it is still a matter of conditioning. As William of Ockham put it—see, I've just appealed to an authority—*entities are not to be multiplied beyond necessity.* So who needs concepts, especially concepts which are immaterial things? Why not just consider concepts as kinds of symbols? For instance, the concept *man* would be a class of synonymous expressions: "rational animal" would, for example, be a member of this class.

MATT: But you just spoke of the class of synonymous expressions. And aren't classes abstract or immaterial objects? The class-of-dogs doesn't bark?

PHIL: Good point! But we could treat classes here as predicates, linguistic expressions of a certain kind. I admit there are controversial questions. We are knee-deep in the problem of universals. However, I don't think any of this will do you any good. You might wind up showing that sophisticated computers are not material things, that they have some spiritual element. If they can pass agreed-on performance tests for understanding, then how can you avoid attributing understanding to computers?

MATT: I would simply refuse to call anything that possessed an immaterial part a machine. Machines are by definition material.

PHIL: I thought machines were by definition realizations of formal systems or Turing machines. That's what you were arguing before. Remember your mathematical argument from Gödel and Church. There is no reason why realizations of formal systems of TMs need to be material. It might be a natural assumption to make, but it is not a necessary one. You seem to have retreated from your abstract, mathematical definition of machine.

MATT: OK. Let's cut to the chase! I'll put my cards right here in front of you. There is an example in the philosophical literature, *your* literature, an example which must have escaped your notice, which I and those I've shared it with find absolutely irresistible. It is the *refutation* of mechanism as we have defined it, in terms of software, or program. As I interpret it, it employs a distinction which goes back to the early part of this century and to the work of Bertrand Russell (who in turn maybe got a little help from G. E. Moore). It is the distinction between knowledge by acquaintance, knowing directly through experience, and knowledge by description, knowing indirectly through knowing the *truth of statements* about some subject matter which may or may not be subject also to knowledge by acquaintance. The example, the thought experiment, comes from a philosopher named "Jackson," I believe, and goes something like this: It's about Mary, a gifted neuroscientist who is locked in a black and white room and perceives the rest of the world through a black and white TV monitor. She knows all there is to know; she has complete knowledge of the neurophysiology of vision: all the neurophysiology, physics, etc. about what a multicolored Grand Canyon sunset looks like, for example. But all her knowledge, her spectacularly complete program, will not prepare her for what things look like when she gets to leave the room. This she will have to learn through experience, through acquaintance. Even complete knowledge by description is not enough. And this is precisely where we humans differ from any possible machine. And I hope you can see this is why your responses to my Robo-Traffic-Cop or other philosophers' responses to Searle's *Chinese Room* thought experiment can never be convincing.

PHIL: Well, I must tell you that I am not unfamiliar with your "Mary" story. In fact, I've given it a lot of thought. I even taught a graduate level seminar largely devoted to it . . .

MATT: How about your cutting to the chase! Do you have a response!?

PHIL: The thought experiment is not as simple as it looks— "complete neurophysiological knowledge." Just what does this expression cover? Maybe present-day knowledge wouldn't allow Mary to recognize colors when she exits the room, but how can we be sure *complete* knowledge wouldn't? Maybe something about her neurological makeup and knowledge of same will allow her to recognize that grass is green and blood is red.

MATT: Well, she might recognize it, make the right identifications. But that's not the point. Now she can for the first time see the colors. Something new has been added to what Mary knows, some knowledge by acquaintance that cannot be guaranteed by any knowledge by description or program. You and your examples still keep trying to bridge an unbridgeable gap. You can't get humanity from machine program. Software, no matter how complex, convoluted, or complete, will never do the trick. So I still say to this example as I've said to your other examples and arguments—magic![13]

Since all these "mathematical," "Turing-like" arguments

13. For a more detailed but ultimately not totally convincing effort to refute the "Mary Example," see D. Dennett's *Consciousness Explained*, especially pp. 398–406.

seem not to have gotten us all that far, why shouldn't we reject some of their premises? The abstract definition of machine was perhaps too abstract (even you might grant that). We mathematicians do like the kind of clarity and precision we get from such abstract characterizations. In fact, we both seemed to admire the elegance of the Church's thesis explication of machine. But I think we might do better to work with a more down-to-earth concept of machine. Given such a concept, I believe I can offer additional arguments to the effect that machines can't understand or think or be human.

PHIL: Surely I have already raised enough problems with your theory of understanding and its peculiar concept of concept to take care of that argument—but I would like you to talk more about your new down-to-earth conception of machine, a conception which guarantees that machines are material and that we are not machines, I take it.

MATT: There's not all that much to it; it's just educated common sense. Machines, at least for our purpose, are simply high-tech digital computers with additional "mechanical" robot-making equipment. Robot-making equipment allows for the imitation of human physical features. But the robot's mind or brain is the computer. This is probably what Turing meant by "machine" when he raised the "Can machines think?" question, and I think we should go back to these roots. I was looking for a quick knockout when I accepted Turing's more abstract characterization of machine in terms of Turing machine. And then you took my abstract characterization and tried to convince me that we humans were after all machines.

PHIL: Aren't we moving backward again? We seem to have given up Turing's *imitation-game* test, or do you have in mind some other test? Perhaps you want to make your contention immune from test altogether. You will only accept a definition of machine that makes it logically impossible for a machine to think, as impossible as it is for a bachelor to be married. That would be one way for you to "win" the argument, but at a very high price. Is there not an empirical aspect to our question? Actually you would have to persuade us to talk your way, to talk in a way in which *machine* and *thinking* are logically incompatible. How could you do this? Would it somehow be too dangerous to do otherwise?

MATT: Wow! You sure have put a lot of words in my mouth. Actually, I do think that it would be too dangerous to permit machines to think, or rather to talk as if machines could think. This would make men machines; it would destroy the conception of man as a person, as a rational, free-willing animal; and that is the very core of our culture and our civilization. We would be, in the words of your behaviorist friend and teacher B. F. Skinner, *beyond freedom and dignity*. We would not be free to choose a plan of life for ourselves, to go about pursuing happiness in our own way, through the use of our autonomous reason. As machines we would be puppets—perhaps better puppets than other animals, but puppets nevertheless. From our input-stimuli and our program-states all our behavior could be, in principle, predicted. (And even if there were room for some kind of random element, this would hardly be the free will of human agency.) Our morality would, of course, bite the dust. There could be no responsibility for puppets. Of course along with morality, religion would also go. So I do see a greater danger in the thesis that man is a machine.

PHIL: Dangerous maybe, but we are after *truth*, or at least *justified belief*, aren't we?

MATT: There is no way we can think of ourselves as machines. We talk about machines in terms of program and state, and input and output. We often know the machine's program because we built the machine. We have a record of input. We can talk sensibly about what the machine *will* do. We cannot talk sensibly about what the machine *ought* to do, or what the machine is *morally obligated* to do. I do admit that we do sometimes speak of others as machines. "I told you Harvey would break his tennis racket. That's just Harvey for you." It's as if we knew enough about his program, his character, and his input history, his history of conditioning, to predict and explain Harvey's behavior quite accurately. But we can never look at ourselves this way. We might treat Harvey as not morally responsible, but we know *we* are responsible. We act; we raise questions about what we ought to do. We don't go around predicting our own behavior. Often we do not know what we will do until we do it, and we don't do it until we choose to do it.

PHIL: Interesting. But couldn't there be machines which would have difficulty thinking of themselves as machines, that is, in describing themselves in the language we use to talk about sophisticated digital computers? Furthermore, as our knowledge in genetics, psychology, and technology improves, how do we know but that someday it might become quite natural to think of ourselves as machines? Someday, for instance, we might find it quite natural to speak of the stimulation of certain fibers in the brain rather than of pain.[14] I'm not saying we would give up our everyday way of talking totally or all at once, but only that this alternative language might gradually take over. It's a possibility, isn't it?

MATT: You are treating this mind/machine question as if it were an empirical one, as if scientific facts could someday lead us to modify our well-entrenched view on the matter. A Euclidian triangle will never be a quadrilateral. And in a sense we *cannot permit* this thesis to be true. Furthermore, you imply that my attitude is intellectually irresponsible. It is not. Even in science, hypotheses are retained in the light of counter-evidence or recalcitrant experience, if the hypotheses are basic enough. You might recall that this kind of conservatism gave us the discovery of the planet Neptune. Well, the hypotheses or principles concerning the special status of human beings are just about the most basic ones we possess. It is only proper that we withhold such principles from test. The very nature of intellectual inquiry, be it scientific or philosophical, presupposes the notions of freedom and responsibility. Progress in a mere science, such as computer science, can never override

14.   This point was, I believe, first made by Feyerabend.

the commitment we have to the uniqueness of man and human personality. So, you see, no single empirical test or set of tests, even something as ingenious as Turing's imitation game test or "progress" in Artificial Intelligence research, can *force* us to give up our fundamental moral principles. Where we have to choose between science and morality, morality must prevail. I believe Immanuel Kant—see, I rely on philosophers other than Mortimer Adler—called it *the primacy of the practical (moral)*.

PHIL: You are really bringing out the heavy guns—Immanuel Kant, no less. You've raised so many new and important issues in your little speech that I hardly know where to begin. At least you have shown that issues in the philosophy of science and moral philosophy have an impact on our mind/machine questions. It is interesting how in philosophy the major problems all seem to blend into one another. What you have done is assume certain positions on these questions, and given the reasonableness of these positions, you have drawn the conclusion that machines can't think, that it is logically or conceptually impossible for machines to think. I suppose what we have to do is examine critically some of the positions you take. I do this not without a certain amount of fear. You have taken us deep into the well of philosophical controversy. I will even admit to having some sympathy for the line you take.

Let's take up the philosophy of science first. You claim that fundamental principles of science are treated as if they are immune to arguments or refutations by experience. Suitable adjustments will always be made somewhere else in order to save the hypothesis. I admit the history of science does at times reflect this attitude, as in the treatment of evolution, of fundamental principles of economics, of the law of effect in operant psychology, and even the treatment of Newtonian physics, at least up to a point. But this conservative approach would make revolutionary progress in science impossible. How could your perspective account for Einstein's overtaking

Newton, for instance? Newton's theory was put to the test and found wanting. It was tested and refuted, was it not?

MATT: The results of the tests never dictated that we give up Newton. We could have made adjustments elsewhere to save Newton. The reason the adjustments were not made was that the scientific community judged that the cost of saving Newton would be too high. I believe the simplicity and the mathematical elegance of Einstein's theory were the reasons for the judgment. There still are scientists and philosophers of science who would hold on to Newton. They are not irrational or crazy; they simply think that Newtonian concepts and principles are just too basic to give up. I, of course, was arguing that fundamental moral principles, principles of freedom and responsibility, are just too basic to allow Turing's argument or any other argument to overturn them. No argument can ever get us to admit that man is a machine, because accepting such arguments would require us to give up fundamental moral principles. The rational thing to do is to prefer the dignity of man over mechanistic arguments.

PHIL: You need a theory of rationality to make that claim stick. We are getting into bigger and bigger questions. In fact, there are some philosophers who would characterize your entire recent approach as irrational. You seem to permit value judgments to override objective facts. If a principle is important, if you are deeply committed to a principle, then you refuse to allow the facts to interfere. Doesn't rationality, on the other hand, require us to subject as many statements as possible, especially the most important ones, to severe testing? Sir Karl Popper holds that science progresses through a process of conjecture (guess) and refutation. On this view, rationality treats nothing as in principle immune to refutation. I guess the problem for us is to choose between competing concepts of rationality or perhaps to come up with a suitable combination. It would be dogmatic of you to insist on the preeminence of your own conservative brand of rationality.[15]

MATT: For the first time, you seem to be a bit unsure of yourself. The philosophy of science is one area of philosophy I know something about. Let me sketch an argument for you that will make you even more uncomfortable. Science involves free rational inquiry. If free rational inquiry were impossible, then so would be science. If man is a machine, there can be no free rational inquiry. If mechanism is to be a scientific result, it must be a product of free rational inquiry, so mechanism cannot be a scientific result. So we can dismiss mechanism as inconsistent with the very idea of science and scientific inquiry.

PHIL: I can see that there is no way we will be able to avoid direct confrontation with the famous or infamous free-will problem. You have argued that if man is a machine, then man cannot have free will. Surprisingly enough, there are philosophers like myself who do not accept this. Machine behavior is admittedly determined: given the input, the program determines output. (A randomizing device doesn't affect the free-will issue. Random events do not make for free will.) Still, some of the machine's actions can be considered free. If you are standing next to a machine and I shove the machine (robot) into you, then the machine's pushing you is not a free act. If the machine's arm falls off because it was injected with a certain substance, then the arm falling off is not a voluntary act. It would be otherwise if the machine were *programmed* to cut off its arm; then the act would be voluntary. On this view, human acts are free when they follow from our characters, when they can properly be said to be *our* acts. Acts which are compelled or forced would not be free. Analogous considerations would have a machine acting freely when it was acting from its program, otherwise not. On this view—a view which by the way has had some distinguished philosophical advo-

15. See Robert Nozick's recent *Rationality* for some of the complexities of this concept.

cates (Hobbes, Hume, Schlick, and many contemporaries)—
determinism and freedom are compatible. In fact, this view is
sometimes termed *compatibilism*. Another name for it is *soft
determinism*. It is the view that is most in harmony with the
way we ordinarily talk, and for this reason it should not be
rejected lightly. The hard determinist holds that determinism
is true and that free will is incompatible with determinism.
Libertarians agree with hard determinists that free will and
determinism are incompatible, but hold that the free-will
option is the acceptable one. You, my friend, are clearly a
libertarian.

MATT: I freely accept the label. I find it hard to understand,
though, how any philosopher, much less a good one, can take
soft determinism seriously. The key question as I see it is
whether a man's character or a machine's program is freely
chosen. If not, how can acts following from character or
program be considered free?

PHIL: I have colleagues in the philosophy department who
also have difficulty digesting soft determinism. They characterize the soft-determinist notion of freedom as too "anemic."
"How could we be free," they ask, "if we have no *ultimate*
control over anything we do?" Of course when I ask them to
explain what they mean by "ultimate control" they do not do
too well. If you think about it, I believe you will agree that
when we speak of free acts, we mean those acts that are neither
coerced nor compelled. Causation is, after all, not compulsion.
I admit that this free-will problem is a tricky one—but why
should we scratch unless it itches, why raise questions about
ultimate freedom and responsibility when in everyday life we
don't see the need to raise them at all?[16] At any rate, I prefer
David Hume to Spinoza and B. F. Skinner any day.

MATT: I'm disappointed. I thought philosophers were supposed to confront these deep questions.

16.   For a discussion of the problem of free will, see the dialogue devoted
to this subject in the Hackett dialogue series: Clifford Williams, *Free Will
and Determinism* (Indianapolis: Hackett Publishing Co., 1980).

PHIL: I don't think we can fairly be asked at this point to resolve such outstanding philosophical problems as the free-will problem. We would have to talk at least another day to resolve them.

MATT: So I guess we cannot resolve our mind/machine problem either. It looks as though we've reached a dead end. So Stu and I might be right about that rotten *Fischkov*, after all.

PHIL: Don't be so quick to give up. I've got one more line of argument I'd like to try out on you.

MATT: Shoot.

PHIL: This new line of argument is similar in some respects to the imitation game. It involves a kind of experiment.[17] We construct as sophisticated a robot as we can. We attempt to program the robot to use English in the way we English-speaking humans use English. This could produce some difficulty, since we may not know English well enough to formulate rules adequate to convey a mastery of the language. The alternative would be to construct something like Turing's child machine and have it learn the language not by explicit rules but by experience, by exposure to the contingencies, as B. F. Skinner would say. (This is the way a native speaker learns the language.) Assuming success with this effort, we program our robot always to tell the truth, never to lie. It could still, of course, be wrong. We then ask our robot such questions as Do you think? Do you have feelings? Are you conscious? On the basis of these we can determine precisely the relation between mind and machine.

MATT: Of course your robot might not be able to answer the questions. What would you do then?

PHIL: I'd have to shop around for a better robot.

MATT: Maybe the questions are simply unanswerable for a robot.

17. After a suggestion of Michael Scriven.

PHIL: If that's the case, this might be enough to distinguish man from machine.

MATT: And what would you do if the machines answered No to these questions? Wouldn't you be tempted to treat the No answer as a sign that you haven't got the robot you want, that you need an improved model? I can't see how you'd ever take No for an answer. And even if it answered Yes. . .

PHIL: What do you think of my crucial experiment?

MATT: I think there are too many ifs about it, such as the mastery of English and the difficulty of interpreting negative, noncommittal, or positive answers. Intriguing idea, though—having a machine resolve the mind/machine problem. If this is the best you can do at this point, then clearly you are running out of steam. I ran out of steam a while ago.

At this point I'm a little confused about things. When we began our discussion I was quite sure that there was an unbridgeable gap between man and machine. I had discussed the matter with some of my mathematician and computer-scientist friends and we agreed that man was inimitable. I admit that some of us believed this on religious grounds, but most of us were especially convinced by the Gödel-Church-Lucas argument. Now all of my arguments have been deflated, at least to some degree, and you've even made use of some of my technical concepts. Still, it's not that you've demonstrated the truth of the mechanist position. It's not, in other words, that *I know* my position is wrong and yours right. What I know now is that I did not know what I thought I knew. What confuses me somewhat is that you brought me to this apparently without knowing the correct position on the man/machine question yourself.

PHIL: You are certainly right about my not knowing the right answer. This has clearly come out in our discussion. If I know anything—and of course I do not claim to be the only one to know it—it is how to ask questions and how to argue; how to adduce reasons for and against positions. We all know a lot more about our question than we knew before. That shows you can know a lot about a question without knowing the answer. Are we better off for our discussion? You'll have to answer this question for yourself. We at least have an understanding of some of the problems involved in the attempt to relate man and machine. That's more than most people can say. As to why understanding is important—isn't the potential for understanding what makes man (and maybe some machines) so special?

STU: As much as I would like to hear you professors talk even more about understanding, I have to leave. I have a game tonight with another machine, *Capaspassky*. I sure could use a win; I hope *Capa* is in low spirits, that he can't keep his mind on the game, that he makes some stupid moves . . .

Selected Bibliography

I

Anderson, Alan Ross, (ed.) *Minds and Machines*. Englewood Cliffs, New Jersey: Prentice-Hall, Inc., 1964. Remains an excellent anthology of fundamental papers. This is the auxiliary text that best complements the present Dialogue. The papers by Turing, Scriven, Lucas, and Putnam are especially valuable.

II

Adler, Mortimer. *The Difference of Man and the Difference It Makes*. Cleveland: World Publishing Company, 1968.

Delong, Howard, *A Profile of Mathematical Logic*, Boston: Addison Wesley, 1970.

Dennett, Daniel C. *Consciousness Explained*. Boston: Little, Brown, 1991.

Hofstadter, Douglas. *Gödel, Escher, Bach*. New York: Basic Books, 1979.

Hofstadter, Douglas. *Metamagical Themas*. Bantam, 1981. (Sequel to smash hit *Gödel, Escher, Bach*—rich in suggestions.)

Hofstadter, Douglas, and Dennett, Daniel C. *The Mind's I*. New York: Basic Books, 1981. (An important collection of essays with authors' responses, includes Searle's Chinese Room paper.)

Polanyi, Michael. *Personal Knowledge*. New York: Harper & Row, 1964.

Ryle, Gilbert. *The Concept of Mind*. London: Hutchinson, 1949.

Sagal, Paul T. *Skinner's Philosophy*. Washington, D.C.: University Press of America, 1981.

Searle, John R. "Mind, Brains, and Programs," in *The Mind's I*, ed.

Hofstadter and Dennett, p. 3 ff. (Originally "Mind, Brains, and Programs," in *The Behavioral and Brain Sciences*, vol. 3, 1980. Cambridge University Press.)

Skinner, B. F. *Contingencies of Reinforcement*. New York: Appleton-Century-Crofts, 1969.

Smullyan, Raymond. *Forever Undecided*. New York: Random House, 1990. (Not much employed in Dialogue but fascinating supplementary reading.)

Webb, Judson. "Metamathematics and the Philosophy of Mind." *Philosophy of Science*, 1967. [Inspiration for much of the argument in the Dialogue.]

Wittgenstein, Ludwig. *The Blue and Brown Books*. Oxford: Blackwell, 1969.

Wittgenstein, Ludwig. *Philosophical Investigations*. Oxford: Blackwell, 1972.